50 ENGLISH PHRASES

Catherine Bruzzone & Susan Martineau

Illustrations by Leighton Noyes

Contents

Special note for learners!

The key English phrases you will learn are numbered on each spread. There are also extra words you will need for the activities. By the end of the book you will know 50 ENGLISH PHRASES and lots of useful English words. There is a summary of all these at the back of the book.

Listen to the audio on our website!

Scan the QR code on the back cover of this book with the camera app on your smartphone or tablet. Contact us on books@bsmall.co.uk if you need any support with this.

Hello!

Have some fun saying hello and goodbye in English. You need to match the right greeting to the pictures, according to the time of day illustrated. Say the correct phrase out loud. You can check your answers on page 32.

1

Hello, good morning

2

Goodbye

3

Good evening

4

Goodnight

Words to Know

Hi!   see you soon

day   evening   night

My name is...

Ask your friends or family to play this naming game with you. One person needs to be blindfolded and twirled round. They then have to 'find' someone and ask **What's your name?** The person answers **My name is...** and says **And you?** Take it in turns to be the 'finder'. You could all choose an English name!

5

What's your name?

6

My name is...

Choose a Name

Sam	Alex	William	Isabel
James	Emma	Charlotte	Alice

How old are you?

You will need two dice for this game. One person throws them and the other asks **How old are you?** The dice thrower answers **I am...
years old**, putting in the number the dice add up to.
Take it in turns.

8 How old are you?

9 I am nine years old

10

Happy birthday!

Numbers! Numbers!

1	one	7	seven
2	two	8	eight
3	three	9	nine
4	four	10	ten
5	five	11	eleven
6	six	12	twelve

Look at the numbers on the inside front cover if you want to ask some older people their ages!

How are you?

Cut out a circle of paper or card. Draw a smiley face on one side and a sad one on the other. Ask a friend **How are you?** as you show them one of the faces. They have to try and give the right answer depending on if it is smiley or glum. Swap round so that you can practise too.

Words to Know

awful   very well   so-so

quite well   thank you/thanks

Where is...?

Find all of the items in the **Words to Know** list and put them on a tray. Practise saying the English words for them. Now close your eyes while a friend takes one item off the tray. (Cover up the English words too.) You then have to ask **Where is...?** whatever the missing thing is! Your friend will either say **Here is the...** or **Try again!** Take it in turns to have a go at remembering.

14 Where is...?

15 Here is the...

Words to Know

book	colour pencil	pen
ruler	pencil	glue
rubber	paper	

What is it?

Look at this outdoor scene and practise saying the English words. Then ask some friends or your family to play a drawing game with you. You each take it in turns to draw one of the named items and ask **What is it?** Everyone else has to try and say what it is from the drawing (and without looking at the English words).
They say **It's a...**.

17

What is it?

girl

bicycle

Here's the family

Spot the family! Look at page 15. Which four people are members of the same family? Point them out and say **Here's the son** or **Here's the daughter**. Use other words from **Words to Know** with **Here's the** too. When you have found the whole family you can say **Here's the family**. Check your answers on page 32.

19 Here's the son

20 Here's the daughter

21 Here's the family

Here are the parents
You say **Here's the daughter** (singular) but **Here <u>are</u> the parents** (plural).

Words to Know

mother/mum	brother	grandmother
father/dad	sister	grandfather
parents	baby	

I like...

Have a look at this picture and try to learn the English words for everything. Then choose four things you like and four you don't like. Practise saying if you like them or not by using the phrases **I like…** and **I don't like….** For example, **I like flowers** or **I don't like mosquitos**. Practise with a friend and take turns.

cats

sun

trees

rain

ducks

pigs

spiders

dogs

17

Where do you live?

The children in the pictures are telling us where they live. Practise saying the phrases. Then cut out four pieces of paper to cover speech bubbles 25-28 and number them from 1 to 4. Ask a friend or adult to call out **one**, **two**, **three** or **four** and say **Where do you live?** You have to try and remember how to say where you live according to the scene next to the number.

24 Where do you live?

25 I live in a house

26 I live in an apartment

27

I live in
town

28

I live in
the country

19

I would like...

Have some fun with this English shopping game for two or more people. Look at the shopping list and practise the words. The first player says **I would like some apples, please** and then points at the next thing on the list, the strawberries, on the market stall. The next player has to add them to the phrase, saying **I would like some apples and some strawberries, please**. Each player adds another thing to the list and the winner is the first one to say the whole list correctly. Then you can shout **That's all, thanks.**

The Shopping List

some apples

some strawberries

some bananas

some grapes

some carrots

some potatoes

some tomatoes

some salad/lettuce

A glass of water, please

It's time to eat so have a go at asking for food and drink in English. You can ask a friend or adult to say **What would you like?** All you need to do is choose something tasty from the menu and add **please**. You might also like to say **I'm hungry** or **I'm thirsty**.

A glass of water, please

Menu

an orange juice	some fruit
a glass of water	some bread
a glass of milk	some ham
a piece of cake	some cheese
some crisps	a yogurt

What do you want to do?

You need two or more people to play this acting game. Read the phrases and then cover them up. One of you asks **What do you want to do?** and acts out one of the activities. The other player, or players, answer **I want to...** whatever they think the activity is. Take it in turns to be the actor.

36 What do you want to do?

37 I want to watch TV

38 I want to play football

39 I want to cycle

40 I want to go swimming

Words to Know

Do you want to...?

Yes, I'd like to

No thanks

25

What colour is it?

Here's a fun game to help you practise colours in English with your friends or family. You will need a die and some counters. When you land on a square all the other players shout **What colour is it?** You say **My favourite colour is red** or whatever colour you have landed on. If you get the answer wrong you miss a turn. Good luck!

41

What colour is it?

START

FINISH

42

What's your favourite colour?

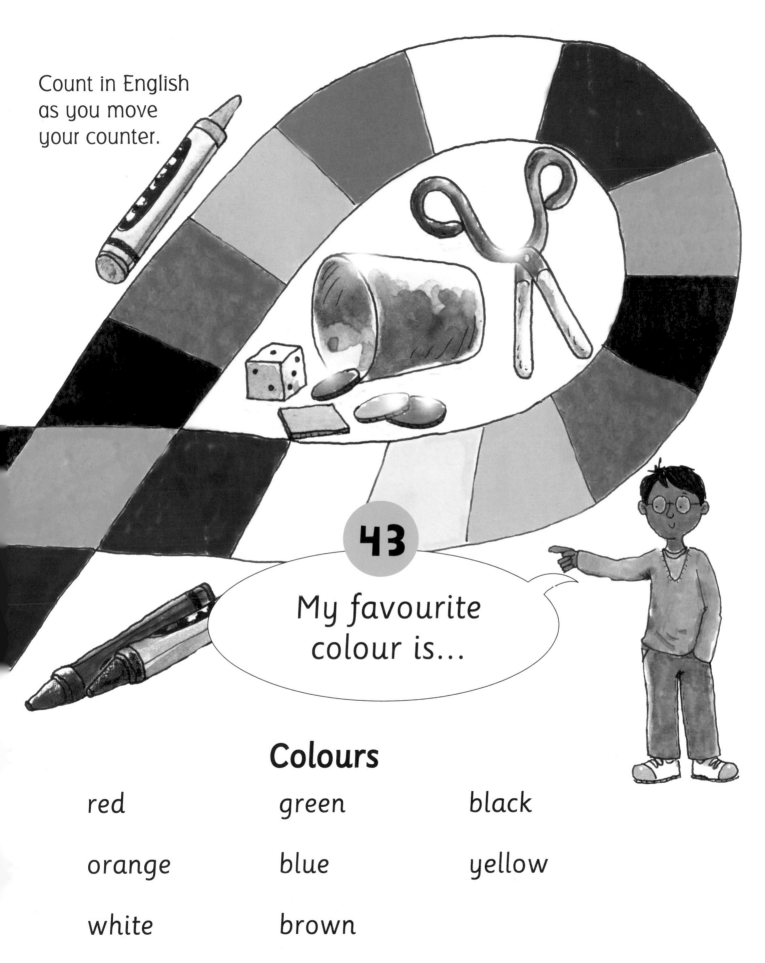

Count in English as you move your counter.

43

My favourite colour is...

Colours

red	green	black
orange	blue	yellow
white	brown	

Where are you going?

These children are all dressed for their holidays. See if you can match the right phrases to the children. Say **Where are you going?** and then choose the right answering phrase. Practise saying this out loud too. Check your answers on page 32.

44 Where are you going?

45 I'm going to the beach

46 I'm going to the country

47 I'm going to the mountains

48 I'm going to town

Words to Know

On holiday

Have a good journey!

I'm wearing...

It's time to get dressed – in English! Have a look at the first picture and say **I'm wearing small trousers**. Now look at the second picture and describe the difference in the trousers. Say **I'm wearing big trousers**. Carry on describing the differences between the clothes on page 31. You'll need to use the **Words to Know**. You can check the answers on page 32.

49 I'm wearing small trousers

50 I'm wearing big trousers

Big or small?

You say **small trousers** and **big trousers** (plural)
but <u>**a small cap**</u> and <u>**a big cap**</u> (singular).

Words to Know

trousers	a T-shirt	a skirt
a coat	a cap	a sweatshirt
big	small	

Answers

Here are the answers to the activities on pages 2-3, 14-15, 28-29 and 30-31.

pages 2-3

4 Goodnight

2 Goodbye

1 Hello, good morning

3 Good evening

pages 14-15

Here's the mother/mum

Here's the grandfather

Here's the daughter/sister

Here's the son/brother

pages 28-29

47 I'm going to the mountains

45 I'm going to the beach

48 I'm going to town

46 I'm going to the country

pages 30-31

I'm wearing a big coat

I'm wearing a big T-shirt

I'm wearing a big skirt

I'm wearing a big sweatshirt

I'm wearing a big cap

I'm wearing a small coat

I'm wearing a small T-shirt

I'm wearing a small skirt

I'm wearing a small sweatshirt

I'm wearing a small cap

50 English Phrases

1 Hello, good morning
2 Goodbye
3 Good evening
4 Goodnight
5 What's your name?
6 My name is…
7 And you?
8 How old are you?
9 I am nine years old
10 Happy birthday!
11 How are you?
12 I'm fine, thanks
13 I'm not so well
14 Where is…?
15 Here is the…
16 Try again!
17 What is it?
18 It's a…
19 Here's the son
20 Here's the daughter
21 Here's the family
22 I like...
23 I don't like...
24 Where do you live?
25 I live in a house

26 I live in an apartment
27 I live in town
28 I live in the country
29 I would like…
30 Please
31 That's all, thanks
32 What would you like?
33 I'm hungry
34 I'm thirsty
35 A glass of water, please
36 What do you want to do?
37 I want to watch TV
38 I want to play football
39 I want to cycle
40 I want to go swimming
41 What colour is it?
42 What's your favourite colour?
43 My favourite colour is...
44 Where are you going?
45 I'm going to the beach
46 I'm going to the country
47 I'm going to the mountains
48 I'm going to town
49 I'm wearing small trousers
50 I'm wearing big trousers